thank you

Dear Friends

Thank you for choosing our book. I hope that this book serves you and your family well. If you have found value in this book, please consider leaving us a review on amazon. It would be very much appreciated.

Adam Freeman

How to Use this Book

To get a complete idea of how to use this book, please read the directions below and follow all of the steps for each writing prompt:

- Read the article and writing prompt.

- Refer to the essay writing cheat sheet.

- Write your multi-paragraph essay following the cheat sheet as a guide.

Expository Writing

Expositoty Writing Cheat Sheet

Paragraph 1: Introduction
- Restate the prompt
- Write brief explanations of ideas you will explore later in the essay.

Paragraph 2: Reason 1
- Write a topic sentence explaining the main idea of the paragraph.
- Add three to four sentences about the reasons/evidence that support the main idea.

Paragraph 3: Reason 2
- Write a topic sentence explaining the main idea of the paragraph.
- Add three to four sentences about the reasons/evidence that support the main idea.

Paragraph 4: Closing Paragraph
- Restate the prompt.
- Add any final thoughts or opinions about the topic.

Animal Helpers

Throughout history, humans have relied on animals for many different purposes. From providing food and clothing to serving as transportation, animals have been an important part of our lives. Here are some of the most useful animals to humans in the past and present.

Dogs have been man's best friend for thousands of years. They have been used for hunting, guarding, and as loyal companions. Dogs have also been trained to help people with disabilities or medical conditions, such as guiding the blind or alerting their owners to seizures.

Horses have also been an important animal to humans. They were used as transportation before cars were invented, and are still used for recreational activities such as horseback riding and racing. Horses were also used for plowing fields and pulling heavy loads.

Cows have been an important source of food for humans for thousands of years. They provide meat, milk, and leather. Cows are also used for plowing fields and pulling carts.

Chickens are another useful animal for humans. They provide eggs and meat, and can also be used for their feathers and bones. Chickens are also easy to raise, making them a popular animal for small farms and backyard flocks.

In conclusion, animals have been a critical part of human life for many years. Dogs, horses, cows, and chickens have been among the most useful animals to humans, providing transportation, food, and companionship. Humans have a responsibility to treat these animals with kindness and respect, and to ensure their welfare is a priority.

Writing Prompt

What two animals are the most useful to humans and why?

_____

_____

_____

_____

_____

_____

_____

_____

_____

_____

_____

_____

_____

Expositoty Writing Cheat Sheet

Paragraph 1: Introduction
- Restate the prompt
- Write brief explanations of ideas you will explore later in the essay.

Paragraph 2: Reason 1
- Write a topic sentence explaining the main idea of the paragraph.
- Add three to four sentences about the reasons/evidence that support the main idea.

Paragraph 3: Reason 2
- Write a topic sentence explaining the main idea of the paragraph.
- Add three to four sentences about the reasons/evidence that support the main idea.

Paragraph 4: Closing Paragraph
- Restate the prompt.
- Add any final thoughts or opinions about the topic.

Tech and Us

Technology has changed the way we live our lives. From smartphones and computers to household appliances, technology has made our daily lives easier and more convenient. Here are some ways in which technology helps people in their daily lives.

First, technology makes communication easier. With smartphones and computers, people can stay in touch with family and friends no matter where they are in the world. This means that people can talk to loved ones who live far away, or keep in touch with friends they don't get to see very often.

Technology also makes learning and education more accessible. With the internet, people can access a wealth of information at their fingertips. This means that students can learn from online resources and teachers can use technology to enhance their lessons.

Another way technology helps people is by making everyday tasks easier. For example, washing machines and dishwashers make doing laundry and washing dishes much simpler than they used to be. Smart home devices like thermostats and lighting systems allow people to control their homes from their smartphones.

In addition, technology makes entertainment more accessible. With streaming services like Netflix and Spotify, people can watch movies and listen to music whenever they want. This means that people can enjoy their favorite shows and songs on their own schedule.

In conclusion, technology has had a huge impact on our daily lives. From communication and education to everyday tasks and entertainment, technology has made our lives easier and more convenient. We should all appreciate the ways in which technology has improved our daily lives, and continue to embrace new technologies as they become available.

Writing Prompt

Write about a type of technology you use and how it helps you in your daily life.

_____

_____

_____

_____

_____

_____

_____

_____

_____

_____

_____

_____

_____

_____

Expositoty Writing
Cheat Sheet

Paragraph 1: Introduction
- Restate the prompt
- Write brief explanations of ideas you will explore later in the essay.

Paragraph 2: Reason 1
- Write a topic sentence explaining the main idea of the paragraph.
- Add three to four sentences about the reasons/evidence that support the main idea.

Paragraph 3: Reason 2
- Write a topic sentence explaining the main idea of the paragraph.
- Add three to four sentences about the reasons/evidence that support the main idea.

Paragraph 4: Closing Paragraph
- Restate the prompt.
- Add any final thoughts or opinions about the topic.

The Wheel

The wheel is one of the most important inventions in human history. It was first invented around 5,500 years ago in ancient Mesopotamia, which is now modern-day Iraq. At first, it was used to create pottery and other small items, but it was soon discovered that it could be used to move heavy objects more easily. Since then, the wheel has been used in countless ways, from transportation and farming to industry and culture.

The wheel has made our lives easier in so many ways. One of the most important uses of the wheel is in transportation. Before the wheel, humans had to carry heavy objects on their backs or on the backs of animals. With the wheel, we can move heavy objects much more quickly and efficiently. Another important use of the wheel is in farming. With the invention of the wheel, farmers were able to create carts and wagons that could carry heavy loads of crops, making it easier to transport them to markets and stores.

The wheel has also had a huge impact on industry. With the invention of the wheel, machines could be created that could move heavy objects more quickly and efficiently, making it possible to mass-produce goods on a large scale. In addition to making our lives easier, the wheel has also had an impact on culture and society. The invention of the wheel made it possible for people to travel longer distances, which helped to spread ideas and culture from one place to another.

In conclusion, the wheel has had a huge impact on human history. It has made our lives easier, and has been used in countless ways. Without the wheel, our lives would be much more difficult and less efficient. The simplicity of this object belies its enormous impact on our daily lives, and we should all appreciate the wheel for its many contributions to human progress.

Writing Prompt

Describe how the wheel has helped people throughout history.

_____

_____

_____

_____

_____

_____

_____

_____

_____

_____

_____

_____

_____

_____

Expositoty Writing Cheat Sheet

Paragraph 1: Introduction
- Restate the prompt
- Write brief explanations of ideas you will explore later in the essay.

Paragraph 2: Reason 1
- Write a topic sentence explaining the main idea of the paragraph.
- Add three to four sentences about the reasons/evidence that support the main idea.

Paragraph 3: Reason 2
- Write a topic sentence explaining the main idea of the paragraph.
- Add three to four sentences about the reasons/evidence that support the main idea.

Paragraph 4: Closing Paragraph
- Restate the prompt.
- Add any final thoughts or opinions about the topic.

Writing Prompt

Describe a science experiment you did and
what you learned from it.

_____

_____

_____

_____

_____

_____

_____

_____

_____

_____

_____

_____

_____

_____

Expositoty Writing Cheat Sheet

Paragraph 1: Introduction
- Restate the prompt
- Write brief explanations of ideas you will explore later in the essay.

Paragraph 2: Reason 1
- Write a topic sentence explaining the main idea of the paragraph.
- Add three to four sentences about the reasons/evidence that support the main idea.

Paragraph 3: Reason 2
- Write a topic sentence explaining the main idea of the paragraph.
- Add three to four sentences about the reasons/evidence that support the main idea.

Paragraph 4: Closing Paragraph
- Restate the prompt.
- Add any final thoughts or opinions about the topic.

A Garden, Step by Step

Building a garden can be a fun and rewarding activity. However, it is important to follow certain steps and provide the necessary conditions for plants to grow properly.

The first step in building a garden is to choose a good location. A location with good soil, access to sunlight, and proper drainage is ideal. Once a location is chosen, the soil should be prepared. This includes removing any weeds, rocks, or debris and adding compost or other organic matter to the soil. The soil should be loosened and aerated to allow for proper root growth.

The next step is to select the plants that will be grown in the garden. Plants should be selected based on the climate and soil conditions of the location. Some plants require more sunlight than others, while others prefer shade. Plants should be spaced apart to allow for proper growth and air circulation.

Once the plants are selected and placed in the garden, they need to be properly watered and cared for. Plants need water, sunlight, and nutrients to grow properly. It is important to water the plants regularly, but not too much or too little. Too much water can cause root rot, while too little water can cause the plants to wilt and die. Fertilizer can be added to the soil to provide additional nutrients to the plants.

In addition to water and nutrients, plants also need protection from pests and diseases. Pesticides and fungicides can be used to protect the plants from these threats.

In summary, building a garden involves selecting a good location, preparing the soil, selecting and placing the plants, providing proper water and nutrients, and protecting the plants from pests and diseases. With these steps, anyone can build a beautiful and healthy garden.

Writing Prompt

Describe the process of planting a garden
and what plants need to grow.

_____

_____

_____

_____

_____

_____

_____

_____

_____

_____

_____

_____

_____

_____

Expositoty Writing Cheat Sheet

Paragraph 1: Introduction
- Restate the prompt
- Write brief explanations of ideas you will explore later in the essay.

Paragraph 2: Reason 1
- Write a topic sentence explaining the main idea of the paragraph.
- Add three to four sentences about the reasons/evidence that support the main idea.

Paragraph 3: Reason 2
- Write a topic sentence explaining the main idea of the paragraph.
- Add three to four sentences about the reasons/evidence that support the main idea.

Paragraph 4: Closing Paragraph
- Restate the prompt.
- Add any final thoughts or opinions about the topic.

Natural Disasters

Natural disasters can happen at any time and can be very dangerous. It is important for people to be prepared for these events to keep themselves and their families safe.

One way to prepare for a natural disaster is to make a plan. Families can talk about what they would do if a disaster occurred, where they would go, and who they would contact. Having a plan in place can help people stay calm and make quick decisions in case of an emergency.

Another way to prepare for a natural disaster is to pack an emergency kit. This kit should include items such as water, non-perishable food, a first aid kit, a flashlight, and a radio. These items can help people survive until help arrives.

It is also important to stay informed about weather conditions and warnings. People can listen to the radio or watch the news to stay up-to-date about potential disasters in their area. They should also know the evacuation routes and shelters in their community.

Additionally, people should make sure their homes are secure. This includes securing loose objects, such as outdoor furniture, and making sure windows and doors are properly sealed. It is also important to have an emergency power source, such as a generator, in case of power outages.

In summary, being prepared for natural disasters involves making a plan, packing an emergency kit, staying informed, securing your home, and having an emergency power source. By taking these steps, people can be better prepared to handle natural disasters and keep themselves and their families safe.

Writing Prompt

Describe what people can do to prepare for a natural disaster.

_____

_____

_____

_____

_____

_____

_____

_____

_____

_____

_____

_____

_____

_____

Expositoty Writing Cheat Sheet

Paragraph 1: Introduction
- Restate the prompt
- Write brief explanations of ideas you will explore later in the essay.

Paragraph 2: Reason 1
- Write a topic sentence explaining the main idea of the paragraph.
- Add three to four sentences about the reasons/evidence that support the main idea.

Paragraph 3: Reason 2
- Write a topic sentence explaining the main idea of the paragraph.
- Add three to four sentences about the reasons/evidence that support the main idea.

Paragraph 4: Closing Paragraph
- Restate the prompt.
- Add any final thoughts or opinions about the topic.

Friendship

Having good friends is important for a happy and healthy life. However, not all friends are created equal. There are certain characteristics that make a good friend.

Firstly, a good friend is someone who is honest. They will tell you the truth even if it is not what you want to hear. Honesty is important for building trust and respect in a friendship.

Secondly, a good friend is someone who is supportive. They will be there for you when you need them and encourage you to pursue your goals and dreams. Supportive friends lift each other up and help each other through tough times.

Thirdly, a good friend is someone who is kind. They treat others with respect and empathy. Kindness is important for creating a positive and inclusive atmosphere in a friendship.

Fourthly, a good friend is someone who is loyal. They stick by your side even when things get tough. Loyalty is important for building trust and long-lasting friendships.

Finally, a good friend is someone who is fun to be around. They have a positive attitude and make you feel happy and energized. Having fun with friends is an important part of building strong and happy relationships.

In summary, a good friend is honest, supportive, kind, loyal, and fun to be around. These characteristics are important for building strong and healthy friendships that can last a lifetime.

Writing Prompt

What does it mean to be a good friend? Use information from the article and your own experience.

_____

_____

_____

_____

_____

_____

_____

_____

_____

_____

_____

_____

_____

_____

Expositoty Writing Cheat Sheet

Paragraph 1: Introduction
- Restate the prompt
- Write brief explanations of ideas you will explore later in the essay.

Paragraph 2: Reason 1
- Write a topic sentence explaining the main idea of the paragraph.
- Add three to four sentences about the reasons/evidence that support the main idea.

Paragraph 3: Reason 2
- Write a topic sentence explaining the main idea of the paragraph.
- Add three to four sentences about the reasons/evidence that support the main idea.

Paragraph 4: Closing Paragraph
- Restate the prompt.
- Add any final thoughts or opinions about the topic.

Writing Prompt

What do you think is the most important invention ever created and why? Use information from you experience.

_____

_____

_____

_____

_____

_____

_____

_____

_____

_____

_____

_____

_____

_____

Expositoty Writing
Cheat Sheet

Paragraph 1: Introduction

- Restate the prompt
- Write brief explanations of ideas you will explore later in the essay.

Paragraph 2: Reason 1

- Write a topic sentence explaining the main idea of the paragraph.
- Add three to four sentences about the reasons/evidence that support the main idea.

Paragraph 3: Reason 2

- Write a topic sentence explaining the main idea of the paragraph.
- Add three to four sentences about the reasons/evidence that support the main idea.

Paragraph 4: Closing Paragraph

- Restate the prompt.
- Add any final thoughts or opinions about the topic.

Animal Adaptation

Animals have developed many different adaptations that help them survive in their habitats. These adaptations can include physical features, such as fur, feathers, or scales, as well as behavioral traits, such as hunting strategies or hibernation.

One common adaptation is camouflage, where an animal's color or pattern helps it blend into its surroundings. This can help animals hide from predators or sneak up on prey. For example, the chameleon can change its skin color to match its environment, allowing it to hide from predators and surprise its prey.

Another important adaptation is the ability to survive in extreme temperatures. Some animals, such as polar bears, have thick layers of fur and fat to help them stay warm in cold climates. Other animals, such as camels, are able to store water in their bodies and can survive in hot, arid environments.

Many animals have also developed unique hunting strategies to help them catch prey. For example, some snakes use their tongues to "smell" their prey, while owls use their sharp talons and keen eyesight to hunt at night.

In addition to physical adaptations, animals also use behavioral adaptations to survive. For example, some animals hibernate during the winter to conserve energy, while others migrate to different habitats to find food and avoid extreme temperatures.

One interesting example of animal adaptation is the giraffe's long neck. Giraffes have evolved long necks to reach leaves and branches high up in trees, which is their primary source of food. In addition, giraffes have a special valve in their necks that prevents blood from rushing to their head when they bend down to drink water.

Another example is the desert tortoise's ability to store water in its body. During the rainy season, the desert tortoise will drink as much water as it can and store it in its bladder. When the dry season comes, the tortoise can go for months without drinking water by reabsorbing the stored water in its bladder.

In summary, animal adaptations are important for helping animals survive in their habitats. These adaptations can include physical features, behavioral traits, and hunting strategies that allow animals to find food, avoid predators, and thrive in different environments. By adapting to their surroundings, animals are able to survive and thrive in their natural habitats.

Writing Prompt

Write an essay about animal adaptation and how it helps animals to survive.

_____

_____

_____

_____

_____

_____

_____

_____

_____

_____

_____

_____

_____

_____

_____

_____

Expositoty Writing Cheat Sheet

Paragraph 1: Introduction
- Restate the prompt
- Write brief explanations of ideas you will explore later in the essay.

Paragraph 2: Reason 1
- Write a topic sentence explaining the main idea of the paragraph.
- Add three to four sentences about the reasons/evidence that support the main idea.

Paragraph 3: Reason 2
- Write a topic sentence explaining the main idea of the paragraph.
- Add three to four sentences about the reasons/evidence that support the main idea.

Paragraph 4: Closing Paragraph
- Restate the prompt.
- Add any final thoughts or opinions about the topic.

Recycling

Animals have developed many different adaptations that help them survive in their habitats. These adaptations can include physical features, such as fur, feathers, or scales, as well as behavioral traits, such as hunting strategies or hibernation.

One common adaptation is camouflage, where an animal's color or pattern helps it blend into its surroundings. This can help animals hide from predators or sneak up on prey. For example, the chameleon can change its skin color to match its environment, allowing it to hide from predators and surprise its prey.

Another important adaptation is the ability to survive in extreme temperatures. Some animals, such as polar bears, have thick layers of fur and fat to help them stay warm in cold climates. Other animals, such as camels, are able to store water in their bodies and can survive in hot, arid environments.

Recycling can also help save energy. When we recycle materials such as aluminum cans and glass bottles, it takes less energy to make new products from these materials than it does to make products from raw materials. This can help reduce energy consumption and reduce greenhouse gas emissions, which can help combat climate change.

Lastly, recycling can help create jobs and support local economies. Recycling programs can create jobs in areas such as collection, sorting, and processing of recyclable materials. This can help support local economies and provide job opportunities for people in our communities.

In summary, recycling is an important way to protect our environment and conserve natural resources. It can help reduce pollution, save energy, and support local economies. By recycling, we can all play a role in creating a healthier, more sustainable future for our planet.

Writing Prompt

Why is recycling important for the environment?

_____

_____

_____

_____

_____

_____

_____

_____

_____

_____

_____

_____

_____

_____

Expositoty Writing Cheat Sheet

Paragraph 1: Introduction
- Restate the prompt
- Write brief explanations of ideas you will explore later in the essay.

Paragraph 2: Reason 1
- Write a topic sentence explaining the main idea of the paragraph.
- Add three to four sentences about the reasons/evidence that support the main idea.

Paragraph 3: Reason 2
- Write a topic sentence explaining the main idea of the paragraph.
- Add three to four sentences about the reasons/evidence that support the main idea.

Paragraph 4: Closing Paragraph
- Restate the prompt.
- Add any final thoughts or opinions about the topic.

Writing Prompt

Write about your favorite hobby and why you enjoy it.

_____

_____

_____

_____

_____

_____

_____

_____

_____

_____

_____

_____

_____

_____

Expositoty Writing Cheat Sheet

Paragraph 1: Introduction
- Restate the prompt
- Write brief explanations of ideas you will explore later in the essay.

Paragraph 2: Reason 1
- Write a topic sentence explaining the main idea of the paragraph.
- Add three to four sentences about the reasons/evidence that support the main idea.

Paragraph 3: Reason 2
- Write a topic sentence explaining the main idea of the paragraph.
- Add three to four sentences about the reasons/evidence that support the main idea.

Paragraph 4: Closing Paragraph
- Restate the prompt.
- Add any final thoughts or opinions about the topic.

Pollinators

Pollinators are important insects and animals that play a crucial role in our environment. They help plants reproduce by transferring pollen from the male part of the plant to the female part. Without pollinators, many plants would not be able to produce fruits and seeds, which could have a big impact on our food supply and the health of our ecosystems.

One of the most important pollinators is the bee. Bees are able to transfer pollen from flower to flower as they collect nectar to bring back to their hives. This process is essential for the pollination of many fruits and vegetables, such as apples, berries, and cucumbers. In fact, it is estimated that bees are responsible for pollinating one out of every three bites of food we eat!

Other important pollinators include butterflies, moths, hummingbirds, and even some species of bats. These animals are able to transfer pollen as they move from flower to flower in search of food and shelter. Without these pollinators, many plants would not be able to reproduce, which could have a big impact on the health of our ecosystems.

Unfortunately, many pollinators are facing threats such as habitat loss, pesticide use, and climate change. This is why it is important for us to take steps to protect these important insects and animals. Some ways we can help include planting pollinator-friendly plants, reducing pesticide use, and supporting efforts to protect pollinator habitats.

In summary, pollinators play an important role in our environment and are essential for the pollination of many plants that provide us with food and other important resources. By taking steps to protect these important insects and animals, we can help ensure a healthy and sustainable future for our planet.

Writing Prompt

Write an essay describing why pollinators are important for crops and humans.

_____

_____

_____

_____

_____

_____

_____

_____

_____

_____

_____

_____

_____

_____

_____

Expositoty Writing Cheat Sheet

Paragraph 1: Introduction
- Restate the prompt
- Write brief explanations of ideas you will explore later in the essay.

Paragraph 2: Reason 1
- Write a topic sentence explaining the main idea of the paragraph.
- Add three to four sentences about the reasons/evidence that support the main idea.

Paragraph 3: Reason 2
- Write a topic sentence explaining the main idea of the paragraph.
- Add three to four sentences about the reasons/evidence that support the main idea.

Paragraph 4: Closing Paragraph
- Restate the prompt.
- Add any final thoughts or opinions about the topic.

Writing Prompt

Write about a time when you felt really proud
of something you accomplished.

_____

_____

_____

_____

_____

_____

_____

_____

_____

_____

_____

_____

_____

_____

Expositoty Writing Cheat Sheet

Paragraph 1: Introduction
- Restate the prompt
- Write brief explanations of ideas you will explore later in the essay.

Paragraph 2: Reason 1
- Write a topic sentence explaining the main idea of the paragraph.
- Add three to four sentences about the reasons/evidence that support the main idea.

Paragraph 3: Reason 2
- Write a topic sentence explaining the main idea of the paragraph.
- Add three to four sentences about the reasons/evidence that support the main idea.

Paragraph 4: Closing Paragraph
- Restate the prompt.
- Add any final thoughts or opinions about the topic.

Habitats

Animal habitats are the places where animals live, find food, and raise their young. These habitats can vary greatly, depending on the type of animal and the environment in which it lives. Some animals live in forests, while others live in deserts, oceans, or even in our own backyards.

Forests are home to many different animals, including bears, deer, and squirrels. These animals depend on the trees and plants in the forest for food and shelter. Many animals that live in forests have adaptations that help them climb trees or hide from predators, such as camouflage or protective spines.

Deserts are home to a variety of animals, including snakes, lizards, and camels. These animals have adaptations that help them survive in hot and dry environments, such as the ability to store water in their bodies or to burrow underground to escape the heat.

Oceans are home to a vast array of animals, including whales, dolphins, and fish. These animals have adapted to live in water and have features such as fins or gills that help them swim and breathe. Some animals that live in oceans also have adaptations that help them survive in different depths of water, such as bioluminescent features that help them see in the dark.

In our own backyards, we may find animals such as birds, squirrels, and rabbits. These animals depend on plants and insects for food and shelter. Some animals, such as birds, build nests in trees or bushes, while others, such as rabbits, dig burrows in the ground for protection.

It is important to protect and preserve animal habitats, as they are essential for the survival of many different species. Humans can help by reducing pollution, preserving natural habitats, and planting trees and plants that provide food and shelter for animals. By working together, we can help ensure a healthy and sustainable future for all the animals that call our planet home.

Writing Prompt

Describe the different types of habitats and the animals that live in them.

_____

_____

_____

_____

_____

_____

_____

_____

_____

_____

_____

_____

_____

_____

Expositoty Writing Cheat Sheet

Paragraph 1: Introduction
- Restate the prompt
- Write brief explanations of ideas you will explore later in the essay.

Paragraph 2: Reason 1
- Write a topic sentence explaining the main idea of the paragraph.
- Add three to four sentences about the reasons/evidence that support the main idea.

Paragraph 3: Reason 2
- Write a topic sentence explaining the main idea of the paragraph.
- Add three to four sentences about the reasons/evidence that support the main idea.

Paragraph 4: Closing Paragraph
- Restate the prompt.
- Add any final thoughts or opinions about the topic.

Life Cycles

Butterflies are beautiful insects that come in a wide variety of colors and patterns. They have a fascinating life cycle that involves four distinct stages: egg, larva, pupa, and adult.

The first stage of a butterfly's life cycle is the egg stage. Female butterflies lay their eggs on the underside of leaves, and the eggs hatch into tiny caterpillars within a few days.

The second stage is the larva stage, also known as the caterpillar stage. During this stage, the caterpillar will eat and grow rapidly, shedding its skin several times as it grows. The caterpillar will continue to eat until it is large enough to enter the next stage.

The third stage is the pupa stage, also known as the chrysalis stage. During this stage, the caterpillar will attach itself to a surface and form a hard outer shell around its body. Inside the shell, the caterpillar will undergo a transformation, breaking down and reorganizing its tissues to form the adult butterfly.

The final stage is the adult stage. Once the butterfly has finished its transformation inside the chrysalis, it will emerge as a beautiful adult butterfly. The adult butterfly will have fully developed wings and will spend most of its time flying, mating, and searching for food.

The life cycle of a butterfly is a fascinating process that shows the amazing transformations that can occur in the natural world. By learning about the different stages of a butterfly's life cycle, we can gain a greater appreciation for these beautiful insects and the important role they play in our ecosystem.

Writing Prompt

Describe the life cycle of a butterfly and why
each step in the cycle is important.

_____

_____

_____

_____

_____

_____

_____

_____

_____

_____

_____

_____

_____

_____

Expositoty Writing Cheat Sheet

Paragraph 1: Introduction
- Restate the prompt
- Write brief explanations of ideas you will explore later in the essay.

Paragraph 2: Reason 1
- Write a topic sentence explaining the main idea of the paragraph.
- Add three to four sentences about the reasons/evidence that support the main idea.

Paragraph 3: Reason 2
- Write a topic sentence explaining the main idea of the paragraph.
- Add three to four sentences about the reasons/evidence that support the main idea.

Paragraph 4: Closing Paragraph
- Restate the prompt.
- Add any final thoughts or opinions about the topic.

Renewable Energy

Renewable energy is energy that is derived from natural resources that are replenished over time, and it offers several benefits over non-renewable energy sources like fossil fuels. There are different types of renewable energy sources, and each has its unique advantages. Let's take a closer look at some of the renewable energy sources and why they are good for the environment.

Solar Energy

Solar energy is one of the most popular renewable energy sources globally. It is derived from the sun's radiation and can be harnessed through solar panels. Solar energy is clean, abundant, and does not produce greenhouse gas emissions. In addition, solar panels can be installed on roofs, reducing the need for land use.

Wind Energy

Wind energy is another type of renewable energy that is becoming increasingly popular worldwide. It is derived from the wind's movement and is harnessed through wind turbines. Wind energy is clean, sustainable, and does not produce greenhouse gas emissions. Wind turbines can be installed on land or offshore, providing energy for remote areas or regions with limited land space.

Hydro Energy

Hydro energy is derived from the movement of water and is harnessed through hydroelectric dams. It is a clean and reliable energy source that does not produce greenhouse gas emissions. However, hydroelectric dams can have environmental impacts like altering the natural flow of rivers and affecting the habitat of aquatic life.

Geothermal Energy

Geothermal energy is derived from the Earth's heat and is harnessed through geothermal plants. It is a clean, reliable, and sustainable energy source that does not produce greenhouse gas emissions. However, geothermal energy is limited to areas with geothermal activity, making it less accessible than other renewable energy sources.

Biomass Energy

Biomass energy is derived from organic matter such as wood, agricultural waste, and landfill waste. It is a renewable energy source that reduces waste in landfills and provides an alternative to non-renewable energy sources. However, biomass energy can have environmental impacts like deforestation and land use.

Writing Prompt

Explain two types of renewable energy and their benefits for the environment.

_____

_____

_____

_____

_____

_____

_____

_____

_____

_____

_____

_____

_____

Expositoty Writing Cheat Sheet

Paragraph 1: Introduction
- Restate the prompt
- Write brief explanations of ideas you will explore later in the essay.

Paragraph 2: Reason 1
- Write a topic sentence explaining the main idea of the paragraph.
- Add three to four sentences about the reasons/evidence that support the main idea.

Paragraph 3: Reason 2
- Write a topic sentence explaining the main idea of the paragraph.
- Add three to four sentences about the reasons/evidence that support the main idea.

Paragraph 4: Closing Paragraph
- Restate the prompt.
- Add any final thoughts or opinions about the topic.

Writing Prompt

If you could have any job when you grow up,
what would it be and why?

_____

_____

_____

_____

_____

_____

_____

_____

_____

_____

_____

_____

_____

Expositoty Writing Cheat Sheet

Paragraph 1: Introduction
- Restate the prompt
- Write brief explanations of ideas you will explore later in the essay.

Paragraph 2: Reason 1
- Write a topic sentence explaining the main idea of the paragraph.
- Add three to four sentences about the reasons/evidence that support the main idea.

Paragraph 3: Reason 2
- Write a topic sentence explaining the main idea of the paragraph.
- Add three to four sentences about the reasons/evidence that support the main idea.

Paragraph 4: Closing Paragraph
- Restate the prompt.
- Add any final thoughts or opinions about the topic.

Plant Food

Plants are living things that grow all around us. They come in many shapes, sizes, and colors, and they provide us with many essential things like oxygen and food. But have you ever wondered how plants grow and make food? In this article, we will explore the basics of how plants grow and produce food.

Photosynthesis is the process by which plants make their food. It happens when plants use sunlight, carbon dioxide from the air, and water to create glucose (sugar) and oxygen. This process takes place in the leaves of the plant, which contain a special pigment called chlorophyll that absorbs sunlight.

Plants need sunlight to grow. Sunlight provides the energy that plants need to create food. It is absorbed by the chlorophyll in the leaves and used to power the process of photosynthesis. If plants don't get enough sunlight, they may not be able to make enough food to grow properly.

Water is also essential for plant growth. Plants take in water through their roots and use it to create food through photosynthesis. Water also helps plants transport nutrients from the soil to the rest of the plant.

Soil is another important factor in plant growth. It provides plants with essential nutrients like nitrogen, phosphorus, and potassium. These nutrients help plants grow strong and healthy.

Finally, air is also essential for plant growth. Plants take in carbon dioxide from the air, which they use to create food through photosynthesis. They also release oxygen back into the air, which we need to breathe.

In conclusion, plants are amazing living things that can create their food. Through photosynthesis, they use sunlight, water, and carbon dioxide to create glucose and oxygen. Plants also need soil and air to grow and thrive. By understanding how plants grow and make food, we can appreciate their importance and take better care of them.

Writing Prompt

How do plants make food and grow? Write an essay with an explanation and

_____

_____

_____

_____

_____

_____

_____

_____

_____

_____

_____

_____

_____

_____

Expositoty Writing Cheat Sheet

Paragraph 1: Introduction
- Restate the prompt
- Write brief explanations of ideas you will explore later in the essay.

Paragraph 2: Reason 1
- Write a topic sentence explaining the main idea of the paragraph.
- Add three to four sentences about the reasons/evidence that support the main idea.

Paragraph 3: Reason 2
- Write a topic sentence explaining the main idea of the paragraph.
- Add three to four sentences about the reasons/evidence that support the main idea.

Paragraph 4: Closing Paragraph
- Restate the prompt.
- Add any final thoughts or opinions about the topic.

Writing Prompt

What do you think makes a good teacher?
Write about it.

_____

_____

_____

_____

_____

_____

_____

_____

_____

_____

_____

_____

_____

_____

Expositoty Writing
Cheat Sheet

Paragraph 1: Introduction
- Restate the prompt
- Write brief explanations of ideas you will explore later in the essay.

Paragraph 2: Reason 1
- Write a topic sentence explaining the main idea of the paragraph.
- Add three to four sentences about the reasons/evidence that support the main idea.

Paragraph 3: Reason 2
- Write a topic sentence explaining the main idea of the paragraph.
- Add three to four sentences about the reasons/evidence that support the main idea.

Paragraph 4: Closing Paragraph
- Restate the prompt.
- Add any final thoughts or opinions about the topic.

School Dress Code

A school dress code is a set of rules that tell students what they can and cannot wear to school. Some people believe that dress codes are a good thing, while others think they are unnecessary. In this article, we will explore some of the pros and cons of having a school dress code.

One of the main arguments in favor of a school dress code is that it can promote a more professional and respectful environment. Dress codes can help students understand that they are attending school to learn, and that they need to dress appropriately for that purpose. Some dress codes require students to wear uniforms, which can help reduce distractions and prevent students from feeling left out based on their clothing.

On the other hand, some people argue that dress codes can be too restrictive and limit students' self-expression. They believe that students should have the freedom to wear whatever they want, as long as it is not offensive or inappropriate. Some dress codes have been criticized for being sexist or discriminatory, as they may require girls to wear skirts or prohibit certain hairstyles.

Another argument in favor of dress codes is that they can promote a sense of community and unity among students. When everyone is dressed similarly, it can help create a feeling of equality and belonging. However, some people argue that this can also have a negative effect on individuality and creativity, and may stifle students' ability to express themselves.

In conclusion, there are both pros and cons to having a school dress code. While dress codes can help promote professionalism and unity, they may also be too restrictive and limit students' self-expression. It is important for schools to carefully consider their dress code policies and make sure they are fair and inclusive for all students.

Writing Prompt

Are school dress codes benifitial for students? Give examples from the text to support your answer.

_____

_____

_____

_____

_____

_____

_____

_____

_____

_____

_____

_____

_____

_____

_____

Expositoty Writing Cheat Sheet

Paragraph 1: Introduction
- Restate the prompt
- Write brief explanations of ideas you will explore later in the essay.

Paragraph 2: Reason 1
- Write a topic sentence explaining the main idea of the paragraph.
- Add three to four sentences about the reasons/evidence that support the main idea.

Paragraph 3: Reason 2
- Write a topic sentence explaining the main idea of the paragraph.
- Add three to four sentences about the reasons/evidence that support the main idea.

Paragraph 4: Closing Paragraph
- Restate the prompt.
- Add any final thoughts or opinions about the topic.

Writing Prompt

If you could change one thing about your school, what would you change? Explain why.

_____

_____

_____

_____

_____

_____

_____

_____

_____

_____

_____

_____

_____

_____

Expositoty Writing Cheat Sheet

Paragraph 1: Introduction
- Restate the prompt
- Write brief explanations of ideas you will explore later in the essay.

Paragraph 2: Reason 1
- Write a topic sentence explaining the main idea of the paragraph.
- Add three to four sentences about the reasons/evidence that support the main idea.

Paragraph 3: Reason 2
- Write a topic sentence explaining the main idea of the paragraph.
- Add three to four sentences about the reasons/evidence that support the main idea.

Paragraph 4: Closing Paragraph
- Restate the prompt.
- Add any final thoughts or opinions about the topic.

How to Resolve Conflict

Conflict is an inevitable part of life, and learning how to resolve conflicts is an essential skill that can help children navigate relationships with their peers, teachers, and family members. Conflict resolution involves identifying the problem, listening to each other's perspectives, and finding a solution that works for everyone. In this article, we will explore some conflict resolution strategies that can help fourth-graders develop positive relationships and resolve conflicts effectively.

One important strategy for conflict resolution is active listening. Active listening involves paying attention to the person speaking, asking questions to clarify their position, and summarizing what you have heard to ensure that you understand their point of view. This helps both parties feel heard and understood, which is essential for resolving conflicts effectively.

Another strategy is using "I" statements instead of "you" statements. Using "you" statements can feel accusatory and put the other person on the defensive, which can make resolving the conflict more difficult. Using "I" statements, on the other hand, helps you express your feelings and concerns without blaming the other person. For example, instead of saying "You always make me mad," you could say "I feel angry when you do that."

It's also important to stay calm and avoid escalating the conflict. This means avoiding name-calling, yelling, or getting physical. If you feel yourself getting angry or upset, take a break and come back to the conversation when you feel calmer.

Another strategy for resolving conflicts is brainstorming solutions together. This involves coming up with multiple options for resolving the conflict and then choosing the solution that works best for everyone. Brainstorming can be a fun and creative process that encourages everyone to work together and find a solution that meets everyone's needs.

In conclusion, conflict resolution is an essential skill that can help fourth-graders develop positive relationships and resolve conflicts effectively. By actively listening, using "I" statements, staying calm, and brainstorming solutions together, children can learn to resolve conflicts in a peaceful and respectful way. With practice, these strategies can become habits that children can use throughout their lives to build positive relationships and resolve conflicts effectively.

Writing Prompt

Describe two conflict resolution strategies
and how they could help you in your life?

_____

_____

_____

_____

_____

_____

_____

_____

_____

_____

_____

_____

_____

_____

Expositoty Writing Cheat Sheet

Paragraph 1: Introduction
- Restate the prompt
- Write brief explanations of ideas you will explore later in the essay.

Paragraph 2: Reason 1
- Write a topic sentence explaining the main idea of the paragraph.
- Add three to four sentences about the reasons/evidence that support the main idea.

Paragraph 3: Reason 2
- Write a topic sentence explaining the main idea of the paragraph.
- Add three to four sentences about the reasons/evidence that support the main idea.

Paragraph 4: Closing Paragraph
- Restate the prompt.
- Add any final thoughts or opinions about the topic.

Wild Animals, Wild Food?

Feeding wild animals may seem like a kind and harmless act, but it can actually be harmful to both the animals and humans. Here are some reasons why people should not feed wild animals.

Firstly, feeding wild animals can disrupt their natural behavior and cause them to become dependent on human food. This can lead to a loss of natural foraging and hunting behaviors, and make them more vulnerable to predators. It can also cause the animals to become more aggressive towards humans, as they begin to associate people with food.

Secondly, feeding wild animals can lead to health problems for both the animals and humans. Wild animals have specific dietary requirements that are different from human food, and feeding them inappropriate foods can lead to malnutrition, obesity, and other health problems. Feeding animals can also create unsanitary conditions that can lead to the spread of diseases.

Thirdly, feeding wild animals can damage the environment. When animals become dependent on human food, they may overpopulate and damage their natural habitats. This can lead to a loss of biodiversity and other negative ecological impacts.

Lastly, feeding wild animals is often illegal and can result in fines or other legal consequences. Many parks and natural areas have laws prohibiting the feeding of wild animals, and violators can be fined or prosecuted for breaking these laws.

In conclusion, feeding wild animals may seem like a kind act, but it can have negative consequences for both the animals and humans. It can disrupt natural behavior, lead to health problems, damage the environment, and be illegal. It's important to respect wild animals and let them live and thrive in their natural habitats without interference from humans.

Writing Prompt

Should you feed wild animals? Explain why or why not. Be sure to back up your argument with facts from the text.

_____

_____

_____

_____

_____

_____

_____

_____

_____

_____

_____

_____

_____

_____

Expositoty Writing Cheat Sheet

Paragraph 1: Introduction
- Restate the prompt
- Write brief explanations of ideas you will explore later in the essay.

Paragraph 2: Reason 1
- Write a topic sentence explaining the main idea of the paragraph.
- Add three to four sentences about the reasons/evidence that support the main idea.

Paragraph 3: Reason 2
- Write a topic sentence explaining the main idea of the paragraph.
- Add three to four sentences about the reasons/evidence that support the main idea.

Paragraph 4: Closing Paragraph
- Restate the prompt.
- Add any final thoughts or opinions about the topic.

Healthy Choice, Healthy Outcomes

Good nutrition is essential for maintaining a healthy body and mind. Eating a well-balanced diet with a variety of foods can provide the nutrients needed to support growth, development, and overall health. Here are some tips on how to make healthy food choices.

Firstly, it's important to eat a variety of foods from each of the five food groups: fruits, vegetables, grains, protein, and dairy. Each food group provides a different set of nutrients that your body needs. For example, fruits and vegetables are packed with vitamins and minerals, while grains provide energy and fiber, and protein helps build and repair tissues.

Secondly, choose foods that are low in saturated and trans fats, added sugars, and sodium. These can be found in processed and junk foods, which should be consumed in moderation. Instead, opt for whole foods such as fruits, vegetables, lean proteins, and whole grains. These foods are generally more nutrient-dense and can help you maintain a healthy weight.

Thirdly, drink plenty of water and limit sugary drinks, such as soda and juice. Water is essential for hydration and can also help with digestion and weight management. Sugary drinks, on the other hand, can add extra calories and contribute to weight gain and tooth decay.

Lastly, practice portion control and mindful eating. Pay attention to your hunger and fullness cues, and aim to eat until you're satisfied rather than overly full. Eating slowly and savoring each bite can also help you enjoy your food more and prevent overeating.

Incorporating these tips into your daily routine can help promote good nutrition and overall health. Eating a well-balanced diet can help reduce the risk of chronic diseases, such as heart disease and diabetes, and improve energy levels and mood. Additionally, making healthy food choices can help you feel better both physically and mentally.

In conclusion, good nutrition is important for maintaining a healthy body and mind. Making healthy food choices can be easy with simple strategies such as eating a variety of foods, choosing low-fat and low-sugar options, drinking plenty of water, and practicing portion control and mindful eating. By making these choices, you can support your overall health and well-being and live a happier, healthier life.

Writing Prompt

Explain the importance of good nutrition and
how to make healthy food choices.

_____

_____

_____

_____

_____

_____

_____

_____

_____

_____

_____

_____

_____

_____

Expositoty Writing
Cheat Sheet

Paragraph 1: Introduction
- Restate the prompt
- Write brief explanations of ideas you will explore later in the essay.

Paragraph 2: Reason 1
- Write a topic sentence explaining the main idea of the paragraph.
- Add three to four sentences about the reasons/evidence that support the main idea.

Paragraph 3: Reason 2
- Write a topic sentence explaining the main idea of the paragraph.
- Add three to four sentences about the reasons/evidence that support the main idea.

Paragraph 4: Closing Paragraph
- Restate the prompt.
- Add any final thoughts or opinions about the topic.

Pets

Owning a pet can be a fun and rewarding experience, but it also comes with its own set of challenges. There are several pros and cons to consider before making the decision to bring a furry friend into your home.

One of the main benefits of owning a pet is the companionship they provide. Pets can be great friends and can help reduce stress and anxiety. They can also provide a sense of security and help with socialization.

Another advantage of having a pet is the opportunity to teach responsibility. Taking care of a pet requires time and effort, which can help children learn important life skills such as feeding, grooming, and exercising. This can also help build a sense of empathy and kindness towards animals.

However, owning a pet also comes with some downsides. One of the biggest concerns is the cost. Pets require food, veterinary care, and other supplies, which can add up over time. Additionally, pets can be time-consuming and may require daily care and attention.

Another potential drawback is the impact on allergies and asthma. For some individuals, exposure to pet dander can trigger allergic reactions and exacerbate asthma symptoms. It's important to consider these factors before bringing a pet into your home, especially if anyone in the household has these conditions.

In conclusion, owning a pet can be a rewarding experience that provides companionship and opportunities for responsibility and learning. However, it's important to carefully consider the costs and potential drawbacks before making the decision to bring a pet into your home.

Writing Prompt

Should people get pets? Explain your thoughts
and provide eveidence from the text.

_____

_____

_____

_____

_____

_____

_____

_____

_____

_____

_____

_____

_____

_____

Expositoty Writing Cheat Sheet

Paragraph 1: Introduction
- Restate the prompt
- Write brief explanations of ideas you will explore later in the essay.

Paragraph 2: Reason 1
- Write a topic sentence explaining the main idea of the paragraph.
- Add three to four sentences about the reasons/evidence that support the main idea.

Paragraph 3: Reason 2
- Write a topic sentence explaining the main idea of the paragraph.
- Add three to four sentences about the reasons/evidence that support the main idea.

Paragraph 4: Closing Paragraph
- Restate the prompt.
- Add any final thoughts or opinions about the topic.

Television

Watching television is a popular pastime for many people. However, spending too much time in front of the TV can have negative effects on both physical and mental health. That's why it's important to limit how much TV we watch.

Firstly, excessive TV watching can lead to a sedentary lifestyle, which can have serious consequences. When we sit in front of the TV for extended periods of time, we're not engaging in physical activity. This lack of exercise can lead to weight gain, poor cardiovascular health, and other health problems.

Secondly, watching too much TV can also have negative effects on mental health. Studies have shown that excessive TV watching can lead to problems with attention span and concentration, as well as a decrease in creativity and imagination. It can also contribute to feelings of loneliness and depression, as excessive screen time often replaces social interactions and other forms of entertainment.

Moreover, many television programs contain content that may not be appropriate for all viewers, especially children. Even with parental controls, it's impossible to completely shield children from all the content on television. Some programs may contain violence, sexual content, or other adult themes that can negatively impact children's development.

In addition, watching too much TV can also interfere with other important aspects of life, such as school work or family time. When we spend all our free time watching TV, we may neglect our responsibilities or miss out on opportunities to spend quality time with loved ones.

In conclusion, while watching television can be a fun and enjoyable activity, it's important to limit how much TV we watch in order to maintain good physical and mental health, protect children from inappropriate content, and prioritize other important aspects of life.

Writing Prompt

Should people limit how much TV they watch?

_____

_____

_____

_____

_____

_____

_____

_____

_____

_____

_____

_____

_____

_____

Expositoty Writing Cheat Sheet

Paragraph 1: Introduction

- Restate the prompt
- Write brief explanations of ideas you will explore later in the essay.

Paragraph 2: Reason 1

- Write a topic sentence explaining the main idea of the paragraph.
- Add three to four sentences about the reasons/evidence that support the main idea.

Paragraph 3: Reason 2

- Write a topic sentence explaining the main idea of the paragraph.
- Add three to four sentences about the reasons/evidence that support the main idea.

Paragraph 4: Closing Paragraph

- Restate the prompt.
- Add any final thoughts or opinions about the topic.

Writing Prompt

Write about a time when you overcame a challenge.

_____

_____

_____

_____

_____

_____

_____

_____

_____

_____

_____

_____

_____

_____

Expositoty Writing Cheat Sheet

Paragraph 1: Introduction
- Restate the prompt
- Write brief explanations of ideas you will explore later in the essay.

Paragraph 2: Reason 1
- Write a topic sentence explaining the main idea of the paragraph.
- Add three to four sentences about the reasons/evidence that support the main idea.

Paragraph 3: Reason 2
- Write a topic sentence explaining the main idea of the paragraph.
- Add three to four sentences about the reasons/evidence that support the main idea.

Paragraph 4: Closing Paragraph
- Restate the prompt.
- Add any final thoughts or opinions about the topic.

Team Work

Working as a team can have its advantages and disadvantages. One of the pros is that when working with others, you can combine your skills and knowledge to complete a task more efficiently. Each member can contribute their own ideas and perspectives, which can lead to a more creative and innovative outcome. Working as a team also allows individuals to learn from each other and improve their own skills.

Another benefit of working as a team is that it can foster a sense of camaraderie and teamwork. When team members collaborate successfully, it can boost morale and create a positive work environment. This can lead to better communication and greater trust among team members.

However, working in a team can also have its downsides. One of the cons is that it can be difficult to coordinate schedules and work styles. Not everyone works at the same pace, and conflicting schedules can make it hard to find time to meet and work together.

Additionally, when working in a team, there can be differences of opinion and conflicts that arise. This can lead to tension and disagreements, which can slow down progress and hinder productivity. If team members are not able to work through their differences, it can negatively affect the success of the project.

Lastly, when working as a team, there is also the possibility of one or more members not pulling their weight. This can lead to resentment among other team members who may feel they are doing more work than others. It can also lead to a decrease in motivation and productivity.

In conclusion, there are both pros and cons to working as a team. When done successfully, teamwork can result in a more efficient and creative outcome, and can also create a positive work environment. However, it can be challenging to coordinate schedules and work styles, and there can be differences of opinion and conflicts that arise. Ultimately, it is important for team members to communicate effectively and work through any challenges in order to achieve success.

Writing Prompt

Is it best to work as a team or alone? Use information from the text to support your answer.

_____

_____

_____

_____

_____

_____

_____

_____

_____

_____

_____

_____

_____

_____

Expositoty Writing Cheat Sheet

Paragraph 1: Introduction
- Restate the prompt
- Write brief explanations of ideas you will explore later in the essay.

Paragraph 2: Reason 1
- Write a topic sentence explaining the main idea of the paragraph.
- Add three to four sentences about the reasons/evidence that support the main idea.

Paragraph 3: Reason 2
- Write a topic sentence explaining the main idea of the paragraph.
- Add three to four sentences about the reasons/evidence that support the main idea.

Paragraph 4: Closing Paragraph
- Restate the prompt.
- Add any final thoughts or opinions about the topic.

Writing Prompt

What is the best movie ever made? Explain your opinion and provide a detailed reason for it.

_____

_____

_____

_____

_____

_____

_____

_____

_____

_____

_____

_____

_____

_____

_____

Expositoty Writing Cheat Sheet

Paragraph 1: Introduction
- Restate the prompt
- Write brief explanations of ideas you will explore later in the essay.

Paragraph 2: Reason 1
- Write a topic sentence explaining the main idea of the paragraph.
- Add three to four sentences about the reasons/evidence that support the main idea.

Paragraph 3: Reason 2
- Write a topic sentence explaining the main idea of the paragraph.
- Add three to four sentences about the reasons/evidence that support the main idea.

Paragraph 4: Closing Paragraph
- Restate the prompt.
- Add any final thoughts or opinions about the topic.

Summer School

Summer school is an option available to students during the summer break. While some children may see it as a bummer, others may find it an opportunity to learn new things and avoid boredom. However, the question is whether or not attending summer school is beneficial for students.

On the positive side, summer school can provide an excellent opportunity for children to catch up on missed material or improve their grades in a particular subject area. For students who struggle in school, attending summer school can be an excellent way to get extra help and attention from teachers. It can also provide children with a structured environment that helps them stay focused and motivated during the summer months.

Additionally, summer school can provide children with opportunities to explore new subjects or interests. Some summer school programs offer classes that are not available during the regular school year, such as arts or music classes. This can help students discover new passions and interests.

However, attending summer school is not always the best choice for every child. One of the biggest downsides to attending summer school is that it takes away from the time children have to relax, have fun, and participate in other activities they enjoy. Summer break is an opportunity for children to recharge and refresh after a long school year.

Another potential downside to summer school is that it can be expensive for families. Some summer school programs charge tuition fees, which can be a significant expense for parents. Furthermore, some children may not have transportation to and from summer school, making it difficult for them to attend.

In conclusion, the decision to attend summer school should be based on the individual needs and circumstances of each child. For some, attending summer school can be an excellent way to catch up on missed material or explore new interests. For others, the benefits of having a break from school and participating in other activities may outweigh the benefits of attending summer school. Ultimately, parents should consider their child's academic and social needs when deciding whether or not to send them to summer school.

Writing Prompt

Should summer school be mandatory? Why or Why not?

_____

_____

_____

_____

_____

_____

_____

_____

_____

_____

_____

_____

_____

_____

Dear Friends

Thank you for choosing our book. I hope that this book serves you and your family well. If you have found value in this book, please consider leaving us a review on amazon. It would be very much appreciated.

Adam Freeman

Made in United States
Troutdale, OR
03/04/2024

18205804R00100